Tropical
DRINKS

C L A I R E C L I F T O N

Illustrated by **CATHY HENDERSON**

CHRONICLE BOOKS
SAN FRANCISCO

First published in 1993 by
The Appletree Press Ltd., 19–21 Alfred Street,
Belfast BT2 8DL
Tel. +44 (0) 1232 243074
Fax +44 (0) 1232 246756
Copyright © 1993 The Appletree Press Ltd.
Printed in the E.U. All rights reserved.
No part of this publication may be
reproduced or transmitted in any form
or by any means, electronic or mechanical,
photocopying, recording or any information
and retrieval system, without permission
in writing from Chronicle Books.

A Little Book of Tropical Drinks

First published in the United States in 1993
by Chronicle Books, 275 Fifth Street,
San Francisco, CA 94103

ISBN: 0-8118-1040-2

9 8 7 6 5 4 3 2

Introduction

An air of ineffable glamor clings to cocktails and tropical drinks. Even simple ingredients, combined with wit and sophistication, served icy cold and decoratively presented in special glasses, can create a heady party atmosphere. Potent mixtures of spirits, exotic fruit juices, and aromatic bitters, shaken in a cocktail shaker and served in dainty stemmed glasses, summon up the jazz age and visions of flappers sparkling in beads and sequins and dashing gentlemen in evening dress with slicked-down hair – the smart set celebrating with hectic abandon between the two world wars. Slings, punches, fizzes, and juleps in tall frosty glasses still evoke cool verandahs, palm trees gently swaying in a warm soft breeze, the fragrance of tropical fruit and flowers in the air, and the dazzling technicolored sunset before the sun comes down like thunder in the tropics.

Even though the cocktail was described in an American magazine as early as 1806, and shrubs and punches were made even earlier, the heyday of cocktails and mixed drinks was the 1920s and '30s. Cocktail shakers and glasses of the period were often made in matching sets in clear or colored glass, sometimes delicately engraved. Chrome, bakelite, silver, or sliver-plated shakers can still be found in junk shops and market stalls, sometimes cheaper than the modern versions.

Good cocktail shakers have a built-in strainer, some have a juice squeezer as well, and most have a jigger or measure on top. You may of course shake drinks without one but they are much more fun to make in the real thing. Decorative swizzle sticks of glass are not expensive and look very stylish,

3

but a long spoon can be used just as well for tall drink. Tropical cocktails are always drunk as cold as it is possible to make them, so remember that cocktails shaken but not served with ice stay colder in a stemmed glass as the contents are not warmed by the fingers. The glasses can be chilled as well. Tall, thin glasses are ideal for punches and slings. Many of the old ones are etched to look frosted. Some old-fashioned cocktail glasses are made of colored glass but when the cocktail itself is colored it should be served in a clear glass. A Blue Lagoon is wasted in ruby red glass suitable for, say, a Tequila Sour garnished with a cherry.

A lavishly-equipped bar is not necessary to create an endless variety of drinks, but fresh fruit and bottled cherries are useful for garnishes and a bottle of Angostura or Orange Bitters will last a long time. A few drops in a non-alcoholic mixture will make it seem more like a proper cocktail and everyone can join in the fun. Straws also add color and most people find them amusing. Pink ice cubes served with tropical drinks are made by tinting the water with Angostura bitters before freezing.

Clear spirits such as gin, vodka, and tequila can be flavored at home by steeping flavoring ingredients in them for two to three months or until the flavor is as intense as you like it. Sloe gin, for example, is an old favorite in Britain. Exotics such as coffee beans, pomelo, and other citrus fruit and spices can be combined to create a unique base for tropical drinks. An orange studded with cloves or stuck with a dozen coffee beans pushed into long slits cut into the fruit can be kept in a large jar with a secure lid and covered with spirit, kept in a dark place, then strained through a coffee filter paper,

butter muslin, clean tea towel, or very fine strainer and poured back into the original bottle or a decanter. The peel of lemon, lime, sweet or Seville oranges, pomelo or grapefruit can be inserted into bottles of vodka or gin. The flavor of vanilla, the seed pod of a tropical orchid, goes wonderfully well with rum and fruit. Leave a split vanilla pod in a bottle of rum and use with fruity cocktails.

Measures

The jigger or measure that is most often used is two ounces or about 50 mls. Some cocktail shakers have a jigger which forms the top and there are also double-ended measures. Metal shakers get cold quickly and tropical drinks made as cold as possible should be served straight away. Shake until the outside of the shaker is beaded with condensation and feels icy in your hands. If you don't have either a shaker or a measure, find something that holds two ounces or 50 mls, such as an egg cup or small glass and shake your cocktails in a jar with a lid or even in a teapot. Cocktails are constructed in proportions of the measure but accuracy is not crucial. If you err slightly it doesn't really matter. Solid ingredients such as sugar are measured in teaspoons and tablespoons. A squeeze of fruit means a good squeeze, usually about a tablespoonful, and a dash of bitters from a bottle with a small plastic shaker top means one or two shakes of the bottle.

Rum

No other spirit is as redolent of the tropics as rum. It is distilled from fermented molasses, left over when sugar cane grown in the West Indies is refined into white sugar. Rums vary in color from pale, almost clear to very dark, and the flavors of sugar and fruit range from light and delicate to deep, complex, and mysterious. Some rums are flavored with raisins, plums, spices, bay, bitter almonds, and other secret ingredients. Jamaica and Martinique are said to produce the most highly-flavored rums although, as tastes have changed over the years, they are lighter overall than they were a century ago. Rum is made in Barbados, Cuba, Puerto Rico, Brazil, and Demerara rum comes from Georgetown, Guyana. Although rum is made all over the world for a true tropical taste use rum made in the Caribbean.

Planter's Punch

I measure dark rum
$1/2$ measure lemon or lime juice
2 tsp sugar or sugar syrup
I dash bitters
soda water

Fill a highball glass with ice, add all the ingredients, stir until until very cold and top up with soda water.

Cuba Libre

This is one of the most famous rum drinks of all, immortalized by the song "Rum and Coca-Cola".

---

1 measure rum
juice of $^1/_2$ lime
cola

Add ice to the rum and lime juice in a tall glass, fill up with cola, stir and serve with a slice of lime and a swizzle stick.

El Presidente

---

1 measure dark rum
juice of $^1/_2$ orange (use blood oranges
when they are in season)
dash of grenadine

Shake with ice and strain into a cocktail with a cherry and a twist of orange peel.

Calprinha

A Brazilian cocktail made with Cuchaca, a clear, fruity Brazilian rum.

---

1 lime, cut almost but not quite the way
through, into quarters
$^1/_2$ tbsp sugar
1 measure Cuchaca or other rum

Crush the sugar and lime together in a heavy-bottomed tumbler, and add rum and ice. Serve with a spoon so that the sugar and lime can be mingled to taste.

Key Largo

1 measure rum	1 tsp confectioners' sugar
$^1/_2$ measure grapefruit juice	dash of bitters
juice of 1 lime	

Shake with ice. Strain into a cocktail glass with a twist of lime.

Frozen Banana Daiquiri

A few hours before you want to make this, peel a banana and put it into the freezer. The ice crystals give it an interesting sorbet-like texture when blended with the other ingredients.

1 measure rum	1 inch chunk of frozen banana
1 tsp sugar	several ice cubes or
juice of $^1/_2$ lemon	crushed ice

Blend all of the ingredients in a blender until smooth. Serve immediately in a cocktail glass.

Pineapple Fizz

1 measure rum	$^1/_2$ tbsp confectioners' sugar
$^1/_2$ measure pineapple juice	syphon soda water

Shake with ice and pour into a heavy tumbler or highball glass and top up with soda water – it fizzes better from a syphon.

Gin

Gin was popular in the tropical outposts of the Dutch and English East India companies. It is named for its main flavoring ingredient, juniper berries. Many of the other botanicals used to give each gin its distinctive character come from the tropics. Every maker has a secret formula which may include cassia bark, coriander, cardamom, orris (iris) root, angelica, licorice root, lemon and orange peel, anise, and fennel. A seventeenth-century medical professor at the University of Leiden in Holland is credited with its invention. He developed it as a cheap medicine employing the diuretic properties of juniper berry oil. Genever is still made in Holland but is very different from the English-style dry gins and has fewer flavoring agents.

It is claimed that gin came to Britain after British soldiers developed a taste for what was to become known as "Mother's Ruin" while serving in the Low Countries. Gin production began in London, Bristol, and Plymouth to supply the growing demand. Gin is made all over the world but some claim London gin is superior. It is even made in Mahon, Minorca which was occupied by the British between 1708–1756 and again during the time of Nelson. Pink gins, gin and "it" (Italian vermouth) and "G & T's" are still drunk in all the far-flung corners of the globe that were ever part of the Empire and, of course, the American dry martini is as recognizable a cultural artifact as the Statue of Liberty.

Banjino

I measure gin
I measure orange, mandarin, or blood orange juice
$^1/_4$ measure Crème de Banane

Shake with ice, strain, and serve in a cocktail glass.

Toronja

I measure gin
juice of I lemon
$^1/_2$ tsp grapefruit marmalade

Shake with ice and serve in a cocktail glass.

Tropicana

I measure gin
$^1/_2$ measure orange juice
$^1/_2$ measure Curaçao, Cointreau, or Grand Marnier

Shake with ice and serve with a twist of orange peel in a cocktail glass.

El Moro

Named for the old fort overlooking the harbor of San Jean, Puerto Rico, which means "the moor".

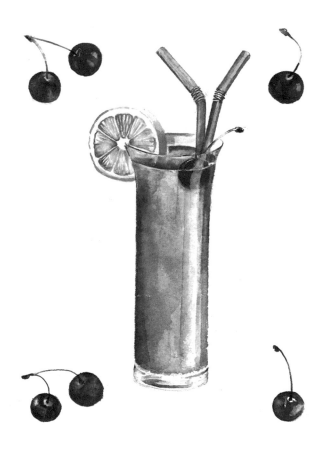

1 measure gin
1/2 measure orange, mandarin, or tangerine juice
dash orange bitters
1/2 tsp confectioners' sugar
1/2 measure dry vermouth

Shake with ice and serve in a cocktail glass with a twist of orange peel
and rub the peel on the rim of the glass.
Variation: Dip the rim of the glass in orange-colored Curaçao
and dip in sugar.

Singapore Sling

This quintessential tropical concoction is said to have been
invented at Raffles Hotel, one of Singapore's distinguished
relics of the British Empire. It was named for Sir Thomas
Stamford Raffles who persuaded his employers, the East India
Company, to sign a treaty with the Sultan of Johore in 1819
after which the sleepy port settlement of Singapore became
the center of British colonial activity in South East Asia.
Singapore became a Crown Colony in 1867 and is now a
thriving independent state.

1 measure gin
1/2 measure cherry brandy
juice of 1 lemon
soda water or lemonade

Shake with ice and strain into a tall glass and top up with soda
water or lemonade. Garnish with a cherry and a slice of lemon
or orange on the rim of the glass. Serve with straws.

Pineapple Julep

---

1 measure gin (or rum)
juice of 1 orange
$1/2$ measure pineapple juice
dash maraschino

Shake with ice and pour into a tall glass. Top up with sparkling wine.

White Lady

One of the most glamorous cocktails of all times. Here is what Molly Keane wrote in her novel Good Behaviour evoking her youth:

"It was glorious then. There are no beauties now like the beauties of the twenties; theirs was an absolute beauty ... on our way to the bathroom we wore crèpe-de-chine and lace boudoir caps – what has become of crèpe-de-chine? or real silk stockings with their transparent clocks, if it comes to that? Or those life-giving White Ladies before dinner before the ball? Not that I am actually against martinis, but I want to go back, I want to soak myself in Cointreau, gin, and lemon juice in equal parts."

$1/3$ measure gin
$1/3$ measure Cointreau
$1/3$ measure lemon juice

Shake well with ice and serve in a cocktail glass.

Bitters

Bitters are alcoholic tinctures of bitter barks, roots, and herbs, the most famous of which and the most widely-available is Angostura aromatic bitters. It was first made by Dr. J. G. B. Siegert in 1824 in the town of Angostura (renamed Cuidad Bolivar in 1846), Venezuela.

The only other bitters most shops carry is the Dutch orange bitters distilled from fresh orange peel. It is sweeter and less aromatic than Angostura. Although bitters do contain alcohol, they are used in such small quantities that they are suitable for flavoring non-alcoholic cocktails. A dash of Angostura added to sparkling mineral water tints it a delicate pale pink and perks up the taste. It can transform a vodka-less Salty Dog into a proper cocktail. Because bitters are regarded as medicinal, it is claimed that they have a tonic effect on the stomach. For example, Angostura bitters were legal during prohibition in the United States.

Aloha

I measure gin
2 shakes Angostura bitters
$^1/_2$ measure orange juice
$^1/_2$ measure pineapple or passion fruit juice
squeeze of lemon
$^1/_2$ tsp confectioners' sugar

Shake with ice and strain into a cocktail glass with a sugar-frosted rim.

Opaline

I measure gin
$^1/_2$ measure Cointreau or Curaçao
juice of I orange
I tsp sugar
$^1/_2$ tsp orange-flower water

Shake with ice and serve in a cocktail or highball glass with crushed ice and straws.

Orange Martini

$^1/_2$ measure gin (or vodka)
$^1/_2$ measure dry vermouth
$^1/_4$ measure sweet vermouth
zest of half an orange

Steep all together for an hour or more, shake with ice and serve in a cocktail glass rinsed out with orange bitters.

Rum and Gin

For tropical drinks made with rum on its own, potent, dark rum gives a stronger taste of the sun, but the lighter rums are preferable for combining with clear gin. The color will be brighter and the aromatic flavor and perfumed scent of gin mixes very agreeably with the slightly sweeter taste of pale rum. They can be used with almost any kind of fruit juice. Or if you enjoy experimenting, add a dash of fruit-based liqueur or fruit brandy and then add a splash of syphon soda and a squeeze of lime.

Silver Jubilee

$^1/_3$ light rum
$^1/_3$ gin
$^1/_3$ lemon or lime juice
dash of orange bitters
1 tsp confectioners' sugar

Shake well with ice and strain into a cocktail glass. Rub the rim of the glass with lemon or lime peel and dip in sugar if you wish.

Diabolini

$^1/_2$ measure rum
$^1/_2$ measure gin
$^1/_4$ measure Cointreau or Curaçao
juice of $^1/_2$ lemon

Shake with ice and serve with a twist of lemon or orange peel in a cocktail glass.

Variation:
Blue Devil Use light rum and blue Curaçao and dip the rim of the glass in blue Curaçao and then in sugar. Shake and serve with a cherry and a slice of lemon on the rim of the glass.

Grenadier

$^1/_2$ measure rum
$^1/_2$ measure gin
$^1/_2$ measure pineapple juice
juice of $^1/_2$ lemon
dash of grenadine

Shake with ice and strain into a cocktail glass, add a cherry and a slice of fruit.

Palm Beach

$^1/_2$ measure rum
$^1/_2$ measure gin
$^1/_2$ measure mixed fruit juice, such as orange,
peach and apricot

Shake with ice and serve in a cocktail glass with a cherry and a slice of lime.

Vodka

Before the second world war the clear neutral spirit called vodka, a diminutive of voda — water — which it resembles only in appearance as it is usually forty to forty-five per cent alcohol, was drunk mainly in Russia, Poland, and the Balkan states. Said to have been made first in Russia in the fourteenth century, it is traditionally served icy cold in small glasses and drunk in one gulp. Sigmund von Herberstein, who visited Russia first in 1517, did not mention vodka by name as one of the variety of drinks set before him at a banquet which included "malmsey, Greek wine, and several sorts of mead" but remarked that "making people tipsy is here an honor and sign of esteem; the man who is not put under the table holds himself ill respected."

Vodka can be made of anything. In Russia and Poland it was made from potatoes, but now is more usually made from cereal grains. It can also be flavored with anything. Lemon, chilli, and wild-berry flavored vodkas are widely available. These are also easily concocted at home. Vodka is made all over the world and Swedish, Finnish, Polish, and Russian vodkas all have their loyal fans. A most unusual vodka, which can't be made at home unless you live in Poland, is Zubrówka, exotically-flavored with buffalo grass which tints it a strange pale green and gives it a remarkable flavor.

Rosy Dawn

---

1 measure vodka (or white rum or gin)
1 measure pink grapefruit juice
juice of $^1/_2$ lemon
dash of grenadine

Shake with ice and serve in a cocktail glass or short tumbler with a cherry.

Salty Dog

---

1 measure vodka
1 measure grapefruit juice or more

Salt the rim of a tall glass or tumbler, add vodka, grapefruit juice, and ice cubes. Stir and serve before the ice melts.

Amethyst

The better the vodka, the more distinctive this beautiful purple cocktail will be.

---

1 measure vodka
1 measure dry vermouth
$^1/_2$ measure blue Curaçao
$^1/_2$ measure grenadine
squeeze of lemon or lime

Shake with ice and serve in a cocktail glass with a twist of lemon or lime peel.

Mint Smash

I sugar lump
5 mint leaves
I measure vodka or rum

Crush the sugar and mint together in the bottom of a heavy tumbler, add the vodka (lime, lemon, or pomelo-flavored vodkas are particularly good), add ice, and serve immediately.

Blue Tango

I measure vodka $^{1}/_{2}$ measure blue Curaçao
$^{1}/_{2}$ measure dry vermouth   squeeze of lemon

Shake ice and serve in a cocktail glass with a twist of lemon peel. **Variation:** Dip the rim of the glass in Curaçao and then in sugar.

Blue Lagoon

A classic cocktail made with the startling blue version of the orange-flavored liqueur made from the dried peel of bitter oranges grown on the Caribbean island of Curaçao, the largest of the Leeward Islands also known as the Dutch Antilles, 37 miles off the coast of Venezuela.

I measure blue Curaçao
I measure vodka
lemonade

Place the Curaçao, vodka, and ice in a tall glass, top up with lemonade, stir until very cold and serve immediately.

Tequila

The agave, also known as American aloe, century plant, or maguey was first mentioned in Europe by Peter Martyr, a contemporary of Christopher Columbus. He probably saw it in what is now Yucatan, the southernmost state of Mexico. Pulque, the sweet sap with which the pineapple-like agave base becomes filled on maturity, quickly ferments, and provides an alcoholic drink which has been consumed in great quantities since ancient times.

Tequila is double distilled from this fermented aqua meil, or honey water. The clear varieties are not aged, but storing in oak casks for a year or more gives tequila a pale golden-straw color and more complex flavor. Tequila is named after the small town near Guadalajara in Jalisco state where most of it is made. The Spanish taught the art of distilling to the Mexicans and it is thought that tequila has been made since the middle of the eighteenth century. However, it was not made on an industrial scale until the two great tequila families, Curovo and Sauza, began to mass-produce it 100 years later.

Añejos tequilas are aged between 6–8 years and are highly regarded by aficionados. Mescal is similar to tequila but stronger in flavor and usually less expensive. It is made from an agave which grows wild in Oaxaca state. The Aztecs used all parts of the agave. The leaf was washed, dried, and smoked, paper was made from the leaves, thread and cords from the leaf fiber. The Apaches made black face paint from the crown of the flower stem after it was charred and mixed with water. Both the Apache and the Papajos are said to have made "fire-water" from roasted agave hearts.

Mariachi

Anyone who has ever been to Mexico has doubtless heard the brassy lively sound of the Mariachi band.

I measure tequila
I measure pineapple juice
dash of grenadine

Shake with ice and serve in a cocktail glass.

Margarita

I measure tequila
1/2 measure Cointreau or Triple Sec
juice of I lime
salt

Shake with ice and serve in a cocktail glass with a salted rim and a twist of lime.

Tequila Sour

I measure tequila
I measure lemon or lime juice
I tsp confectioners' sugar

Shake with ice and serve in a cocktail glass with a cherry.

Brandy

Every country which produces wine also makes "burnt wine", or brandy, from the Dutch brandewijn. In France, brandy made in the small town of Cognac or in the district of Armagnac is called by the name of the place. As with wine, the grape variety determines the taste. Greek grapes make a very different brandy from Spanish sherry grapes. Some brandies are aged in oak casks and even the type of oak used has an effect on the ultimate taste. Many less expensive brandies have an agreeable flavor and most of them are perfectly adequate for mixing cocktails.

Cuban Missile

I measure brandy
$^1/_2$ measure apricot brandy
juice of $^1/_2$ lime

Shake with ice and strain into a cocktail glass.

Bombay Punch

$^1/_2$ measure brandy
$^1/_2$ measure sherry
dash of maraschino
dash of Curaçao or Cointreau
sparkling wine
syphon soda water

Place the first 4 ingredients into a tall glass, add ice, stir well, and top up with sparkling wine and a squirt of syphon soda water. Garnish with a cherry and a slice of fruit. Serve with straws.

Brandy Sour

I measure brandy
juice of I lemon or lime
dash of Angostura bitters
I tsp confectioners' sugar

Shake well with ice and strain into a cocktail glass. Garnish with a cherry and a twist of lemon or lime peel.

Stinger

This is an ideal after-dinner cocktail but packs quite a punch and is not as innocent as the mint hints to the taste buds. It is a drink to be sipped in candle-light, in front of a flickering open fire or in a secluded corner of a dimly lit cocktail lounge.

$^{1}/_{2}$ measure brandy
$^{1}/_{2}$ measure white crème de menthe

Shake well with ice and serve in a cocktail glass or stir and pour over crushed ice in a highball glass.

Bourbon

Bourbon is whiskey, or "corn likker" when it's legal, moonshine when it isn't. In 1794, liquor-loving, tax-hating distillers from Western Pennsylvania decamped into Bourbon County, Kentucky, not at that time a state, escaping from federal troops sent in by President George Washington to quell the Whiskey Rebellion. The rebels found in Kentucky the same pure spring water they had used at home, but when the rye crop failed, they had to eke the rye out with corn and thus discovered that the result was sweeter than whiskey made form rye alone. Dr. James Crow, a Scot, determined to refine the American product, began aging his whiskey in white oak barrels in the 1830s, but the discovery that charred oak barrels further enhanced the taste was also accidental.

There are many stories about the first charred barrels: a fire in a West Indian rum distillery; lightning striking a barn; a distiller too thrifty to throw away a fire-damaged barrel; a cooper burning out the taste of recycled fish-barrels; take your pick. Modern bourbon is, by law, made from more than fifty per cent corn, aged for at least two years in new charred white oak barrels, and must be not less than eighty U.S. proof. However, some bourbons are made from eighty per cent corn and aged for more than six years. Real bourbon drinkers are fanatically loyal to their brand of choice. The taste varies according to how much rye, wheat, or barley is used in addition to corn, the aging, and the proof.

Bourbon Manhattan

I measure bourbon
$^1/_2$ measure sweet or dry vermouth
dash bitters

Stir well with ice and strain into a highball glass and serve with a twist of lemon or a slice of orange and a cherry.

New Age Old Fashioned

I measure bourbon
2 dashes Angostura or Orange bitters
squeeze of lemon

Shake with ice and strain into a highball glass. Serve with a cherry and a slice of orange or lemon, or serve on the rocks and stir with a swizzle stick.

Lynchburg Lemonade

Named for Lynchburg, Virginia, a town in the foothills of the beautiful Blue Ridge Mountains, both famous and infamous in the annals of American history. In 1757 a group of Quakers settled near a ferry landing owned by John Lynch and their town was called after him. During the American Revolution his brother Charles, a zealous patriot, dealt with loyalist Tories in a summary fashion, trying, and sentencing them in his kangaroo court, giving the family name forever to the expression "lynch law" and lynching.

Lynchburg's more glorious hour came during the Civil War when General Jubal A. Early defeated General David Hunter's Union troops there in June, 1864.

I measure bourbon
¹/₂ measure Triple Sec or Cointreau
squeeze of lemon
lemonade

Place the bourbon, Triple Sec, or Cointreau, and lemon juice in a tall glass, add ice, and top up with lemonade. Serve with straws and a cherry, if you wish.

Mint Julep

The most famous bourbon drink of all is the Mint Julep. Here is one recipe though there are many.

I tbsp chopped mint
I tbsp sugar
I measure bourbon
generous sprig of fresh mint

Crush the mint and sugar to a paste in a mortar and pestle or in a small bowl with a wooden spoon, then add just enough water to make the mixture liquid. Fill a chilled metal cup (or highball glass) with crushed ice, pour in the mint syrup and the bourbon and stir. If you are using a metal cup, put it in the freezer until it is frosted. Serve garnished with fresh mint and short straws.

Bourbon Sour

---

1 measure bourbon
juice of $^1/_2$ lemon
1 tsp confectioners' sugar
fresh mint

Shake with ice and strain into a cocktail glass. Serve with a cherry, or a twist of lemon peel and a sprig of fresh mint.

Non-alcoholic Cocktails

Anyone who has ever resolutely stuck to unadorned fizzy water with a wedge of lemon or lime at a drinks' party (one glass of undiluted fruit juice is usually more than enough for most of us) will be cheered by the appearance of a non-alcoholic cocktail, especially one that doesn't look like a "virgin" drink and is glamorous and jolly enough to put a teetotaller in a party mood. A glass of mineral water can just about pass for a gin and tonic but the addition of non-alcoholic ingredients can make it look like a technicolored cocktail.

Fruit juices are less cloying and so much jazzier when they are diluted and a dash of grenadine or bitters peps them up no end. When non-alcoholic mixtures are shaken and served in the same cocktail glasses everyone else is drinking from, no one feels left out of the fun, and the taste is just as exciting as the cocktails that do contain alcohol.

Long Boat

I measure lime juice cordial
ginger beer
fresh mint

Fill a tall glass with ice, add lime juice cordial, and top up with ginger. Add a sprig of fresh mint and a cherry, serve with straws.

Great White Hunter

I measure lime juice cordial
juice of I lemon, lime or passion fruit
dash of grenadine
tonic water

Fill a highball glass with ice, add all the ingredients, stir, and top up with tonic water. Serve with a slice of lemon.

Conga

$^1/_2$ measure lemon juice
$^1/_2$ measure pineapple, passion fruit, or mixed fruit juice
juice of $^1/_2$ lemon
dash of grenadine
dash of bitters

Fill a tall glass with ice, add all the ingredients, stir, and top up with lemonade or ginger ale. Garnish with a cherry and a slice of orange.

Ginger-pine

I measure unsweetened pineapple juice
ginger ale

Place the pineapple juice in a highball or tall glass, add ice cubes or crushed ice, top up with ginger ale, and serve with a cherry and straws.

Mint Spritzer

I measure mint cordial
squeeze of fresh lemon
soda water

Fill a tall glass with ice cubes, add mint cordial and lemon juice, and top up with soda water. Serve with a slice of lemon on the rim of the glass and a sprig of fresh mint.

Spanner

I measure orange juice
dash of grenadine or Angostura or Orange bitters
ginger ale

Place the orange juice and grenadine or bitters in a highball glass, add ice, and top up with ginger ale. Serve with a cherry, and a slice of orange or lemon on the rim of the glass.

Iced "Sun" Tea

Given that iced tea is really only suitable to drink when the sun is shining it is sensible to use the sun to make it. It also allows the tea to be served immediately as no cooling down is required. It is made simply by putting two tea bags per two pints of tap, spring, or bottled water in a glass container with a lid or cloth on top and letting it sit in strong sunlight for about twenty minutes. Serve with ice and decorate with fresh mint or lemon slices and straws. Have sugar lumps and long spoons on hand for those who wish to add sugar.

Any kind of tea may be used but the exotically flavored teas are a nice change from the every-day Indian teas. Try Earl Grey, Lapsang Souchong, Rose Pouchong, or one of the spice and fruit-flavored teas. Herb teas may also be made in the same way – mint, rose hip, and hibiscus, for example, but add an extra tea bag to insure that the flavor will be intense enough to allow for melting ice to dilute it.

Spiced Jasmine Tea is beautifully aromatic and is easily concocted at home. In a mixing bowl stir together loose jasmine tea with whole cloves (about a tablespoon per half pound), 2 cinnamon sticks broken into pieces and a dozen crushed cardamom pods, and an inch of split vanilla bean. Store in an air-tight container. To make sun tea, place the mixture in a muslin bag tied with a long piece of string, or make it in the ordinary way and allow it to cool before adding ice.

Iced Coffee

To be served iced, coffee should ideally be made well ahead of time so that it doesn't immediately melt the ice. You can blend cold coffee, milk, sugar, and ice in a blender for a frothy drink or simply serve coffee and ice in tall glasses and pass round milk, sugar, and long spoons separately.

Use a good high roast coffee and make it very strong as the blander coffees are rather insipid when iced as ice will dilute the flavor. Or try one of the many flavored coffees available at coffee shops. They are especially delicious when served iced and there is a wide variety to choose from – hazelnut, almond, chocolate, amaretto, brandy, cinnamon, vanilla, and chocolate mint, to name but a few. For a really extravagant touch, add a dollop of thick cream and a very light dusting of powdered cinnamon. Serve with long spoons or straws.

To make your own chocolate-flavored coffee, simply add a spoonful of cocoa powder to freshly ground coffee and brew it in an expresso pot. For a Middle Eastern flavor add one or two crushed cardamom pods or a pinch of ground cardamom to ground coffee. All coffee keeps best in the freezer.

Index